MW01610920

Conducting Assessments

Evaluating Programs, Facilities,

Agencies and Organizations

by Bob Frost, Ph.D.

Copyright © 2011
Bob Frost
Dallas, Texas

All rights reserved. No portion of this publication may
be reproduced in any form or by any means, electronic or
mechanical, without written permission from the copyright
owner. Inquiries should be addressed to the author.

Published by
Measurement International
Dallas, Texas   75209

ISBN 978-0-9702471-3-1

Contents

Preface

This book grew out of the realization that assessments are widely conducted by practitioners from many diverse professions, and the need we saw for a simple summary to share principles and best practices across professions.

The early portions of this book cover basic concepts and a few simple distinctions that I find useful, but which are not readily found elsewhere. From there it moves into more pragmatic matters of optimizing the quality of assessments, accomplishing the work of an assessment, and improving assessment processes.

As with our other books in this series (Crafting Strategy; Measuring Performance; and Designing Metrics), Conducting Assessments strives to clarify terminology and summarize basic principles in a practical way.

My most sincere thanks to each of the colleagues and assessment practitioners who critiqued this work and suggested improvements.

–Bob Frost

Part 1

Assessment Basics

- Introduction

- Purpose of Assessments

- Flow of an Assessment

- Check Your Assessments

Introduction

What do safety inspections, school accreditations, wine tastings, financial audits, and scientific program reviews all have in common? They are all types of assessments or evaluations. And there are many other types as well.

Suppose you are responsible for a nuclear power plant. And a similar plant has just been damaged by an earthquake. How, exactly, can you know your plant is safe from such damage? The original design and construction specifications were state-of-the-art. Those who built the plant have given you their strongest assurances. And you know earthquakes are rare in your area. But you also know earthquake damage, if it occurred, could be devastating in every possible way. How can you better know the earthquake safety of your plant?

Like many other industries, the nuclear power industry has developed ways of assessing such risks. But, to carry the

Some assessments are extremely important and we need to know they can be trusted

illustration a step further, how can we know that these risk assessments are good enough? Can the assessments be trusted? How can we know that? Assess the assessments?

Rest assured, we will not get into an infinite regression of assessing assessments, nor into the philosophy of how we can know anything for certain. But you get the point. Some assessments are extremely important and we need to know they can be trusted. That's our topic for the remainder of this book: conducting high quality, trustworthy assessments.

You will find assessments in education, government, nonprofits, business and industry, public administration, research and development, consumer products and elsewhere. They go by many names—assessments, evaluations, inspections, audits, reviews and so forth. Since the distinctions among these terms are not widely recognized across fields, we will simply use the term assessment.

The distinguishing characteristic of all assessments is that they call for a judgment or conclusion about the success, impact, quality, performance, compliance, or other characteristic of an entity. Evidence, strong or weak, is used in making such judgments and usually offered as support for the conclusions reached.

For example, a panel of scientists might assess a research program—its quality and direction, the results it has produced, or the advisability of continued funding. Or an oversight agency might assess safety at a nuclear power plant. Or an accrediting agency might assess a particular college or university. Or a commercial business might assess its program for product development. Pharmaceutical companies might self-assess their manufacturing processes. Assessments are nearly endless in variety.

Internal vs. External Assessments. Assessments conducted by the entity being assessed are usually called self-assessments or internal assessments, and those conducted by outsiders external assessments or independent assessments. Both internal and external assessments have their places. Internal assessments are especially useful to those pursuing continuous improvement in a cost effective way; external assessments are especially useful when objectivity and credibility are paramount.

In addition to pure internal and external assessments, some mix internal and external resources. For example, an external resource might design and provide leadership for an internally-staffed assessment, toward the goal of improving quality and credibility while taking advantage of internal knowledge and keeping costs down.

Assessed Entities. Defining an assessment begins with specifying the entity to be assessed. What kind of entity is it? What is included and not included? Assessments commonly focus on:

- Programs
- Products

- Facilities
- Processes
- Organizations
- Individuals
- Natural environment
- And other entities

The entity to be assessed may be called the focus of the assessment, target of the assessment, or the evaluand. In this book, we will use entity or assessed entity.

Assessed Characteristic. Next comes the characteristic of the entity to be assessed. Is it one characteristic (e.g., safety) or more than one? Some assessments skip this step; we believe that is a mistake. What about the program or process is being assessed? Everything? That's not possible. Skipping this step results in an assessment that literally does not know where it is going. It's much better to define the assessed characteristic(s) up front and design the rest of the effort based on this clear definition.

Characteristics commonly assessed include things like:

- Capability
- Compliance (with laws, regulations, contracts)
- Condition (as in environmental assessments)
- Effectiveness
- Efficiency

9

- Emerging issues or problems
- Knowledge, skills, mastery, competence
- Performance
- Quality
- Readiness for some activity, event, or use
- Relevance
- Results and/or impacts
- Risk
- Safety or security
- Strategy or direction
- Sustainability
- And other characteristics

So, a given assessment is defined by specifying the entity to be assessed, such as a particular power plant, and some specific characteristic to be assessed, such as risk from earthquakes. Some examples are: "Assessing Effectiveness of the Lane County Food Bank Program;" or "An Operational Readiness Assessment of the Bridges Power Plant."

Multiple Characteristics and Dimensions. Oftentimes multiple characteristics of an entity are assessed. For example, in evaluating Federal Government programs the Program Assessment Rating Tool (Office of Management and Budget, 2003-2008) addressed:

- Program Purpose & Design
- Planning
- Management
- Results

It is often the case that a broad characteristic is subdivided into constituent dimensions for an assessment. For example, to assess the characteristic "performance," it might be divided into the dimensions of "effectiveness," "efficiency," and "sustainability" which would be gauged separately and then combined into an overall assessment of program "performance." It is always a good practice to provide a careful operational definition of the characteristic(s) and dimensions being assessed.

"Always set operational definitions at the outset—as you go forward, nothing is quite so useful as knowing exactly what you are doing."   –C. Snyder

Let's pause here and summarize three points about terminology:

1) *Entity* refers to the object of our assessment.

2) *Characteristic* is what we are assessing about the entity.

3) *Dimensions*, if used, are sub-components of the characteristic(s) we are assessing.

11

For example, the assessed entity might be a particular city or county; the assessed characteristic might be readiness of emergency communications; the dimensions might include radio communications to citizens, television communication to citizens, integration of police, fire and other radio systems, and so forth.

Conclusion. Though assessments are practiced in many ways in many different places, they all have in common the one characteristic noted earlier—they all call for some type of judgment or evaluative decision, based on supporting evidence. Even assessments which seem totally mechanical and objective, such as those based on checklists or machine scored surveys, involve professional judgment in constructing the instruments, creating scoring templates, and interpreting scores. All assessments involve some degree of professional judgment.

Yet, if assessments are to be relied upon, they must have certain attributes—validity, fairness, reliability, etc. And human judgments, even those given by experts and based on evidence, do not always have all the validity, fairness, reliability, and other qualities we desire. The overarching goal of all well-conducted assessments is to employ the assessors' knowledge of the topic and, at the same time, guard against the known frailties of human judgments.

Every well-conducted assessment addresses this goal and utilizes specific mechanisms for collecting evidence and making judgments. We can think of assessments as "structured judgment processes" in which we build fences around how judgments are made—how the task is defined, evidence is collected, and conclusions are drawn—to help bring about validity, fairness, reliability, etc. The principles behind these fence-building activities are rooted in scientific method, statistics, cognitive studies, and laboratory studies of decision making.

In the past, various professions have developed principles and best practices for conducting assessments. However these professions have largely been stovepiped—relying on their own principles and practices and gaining little from the practices employed elsewhere.

In this book, we will:

1) Describe what high quality assessments have in common

2) Outline the process of conducting assessments, and

3) Discuss key principles and best practices culled from various fields.

We intend that this concise summary will help sound assessment principles and practices find broader application.

The principles and practices we review will be drawn from diverse assessment situations, yet we believe they apply to every type of assessment. Our intention is very broad in this sense, but readers should realize that we usually have in mind the myriad programs, facilities, agencies and organizations that must be gauged periodically to support their own improvement plans, their contract requirements, and/or decisions by their sponsors.

Purpose of Assessments

Assessment reports usually contain a statement of purpose and, if you look across many such statements, you soon realize that there are only a few underlying purposes for which assessments are conducted:

1) Support accountability, transparency, and/or compliance. Internal assessments and, especially, external assessments are commonly conducted because a person, oversight agency, or funder wants to understand: 1) what is being accomplished; 2) how well it is being accomplished; 3) whether funds are being well spent; and 4) whether compliance with rules, contracts, regulations and requirements is being achieved.

The Federal Government increasingly requires assessments of programs and agencies to help establish accountability and ensure that taxpayer funds are used to good effect. One example of this, noted earlier, is the Program Assessment and Rating Tool, used for some years in rating Federal agencies. State and local governments, as well as the nonprofit sector, are also increasing their use of assessments for accountability purposes.

2) Improve performance or precipitate needed change. Performance improvement is widely cited as the purpose for conducting assessments. Examples range from evidence-based assessments of projects and programs by educators or

15

scientists to "assessment centers" for managerial development.

The careful assessment of strong and weak points is certainly helpful in planning how a project, program, or organization can be improved in the future. Furthermore, when change is clearly needed but things seem stuck in neutral, an assessment can often highlight issues in a way that spurs decisions and gets things moving again.

3) **Improve decision making and reduce risk.** To the degree they are well conducted, assessments provide reasonably objective sources of information for government officials, business leaders, and nonprofit organizations and their funders to make sound decisions. They provide information on current and emerging problems, the assurance that decisions rest on sound bases, and critical information about conditions of risk. Without strong assessments, there is an increased risk of error or unintended results.

In some fields, assessment practitioners speak of two types of assessments or evaluations—formative and summative. Formative are those conducted primarily for improving the entity. Summative are those conducted primarily for accountability or decision making purposes. Of course, here as in other fields, practitioners often intend for their efforts to fulfill more than one purpose simultaneously.

Flow of an Assessment

There is a logical flow in each assessment process. Scriven (1969, 1989) describes four steps in the sequence:

1) Selecting the characteristics and dimensions that will be assessed.

2) Setting standards of performance—defining what is good and not good on the characteristics/dimensions and developing any scales or evaluation tools.

3) Gathering and analyzing evidence pertinent to gauging performance on the criteria.

4) Integrating the results into a final conclusion.

This logic applies to expert assessments, committee evaluations, peer reviews, test-based assessments and all other varieties of assessments. Later, we will expand on this logic as we take a detailed look at the process.

17

Check Your Assessments

You may already conduct assessments—perhaps many of them. If so, you can perform a quick, informal check on their quality with the following checklist. Check the box by each statement that is true in your organization.

❑ Each assessment is carefully planned in advance

❑ An experienced, well-qualified leader is in charge of each assessment

❑ Assessors are appropriately trained and knowledgeable on both the entity and the characteristic(s) being assessed

❑ Characteristic(s) being assessed are thoroughly defined at the outset

❑ Standards of performance for each assessed characteristic are thoroughly defined at the outset

❑ Evidence collection tools are well constructed, with scripted interview questions, specific checklists for field inspections, and so forth.

❑ Multiple types of evidence are collected on each characteristic or dimension assessed

❑ Evidence is analyzed independently by multiple assessors before final consensus

❑ The process, monitored by the assessment leader, assures that extraneous variables (such as assessor biases and personalities) minimally influence the outcome

❑ The assessment report is appropriately thorough and detailed, presenting sufficient evidence to inspire confidence in the result

❑ Assessments gauge exactly what they say they do, nothing more and nothing less

❑ The cost of each assessment is in reasonable proportion to its importance and regarded as a good investment

❑ Assessments are well accepted and the results are nearly always used in making decisions or necessary improvements

❑ Assessments are seen as valid and unbiased by the sponsors and the entities assessed

You've just completed an informal assessment. Your checkmarks say something significant about the strengths and weaknesses of your assessment program. There are many ways to make informal assessments like this one more systematic, more reliable, and more credible. We will be taking up those ways in the remainder of this book.

Part 2

Conducting Quality Assessments

- Introduction

- Three Keys to Quality

  1) The Evidence

  2) The Assessors

  3) The Assessment Process

Introduction

*"Practitioners must remain keenly aware of the context
in which assessment results will be used and the
necessity of having credibility in that context."*
–G. Kaufman

We have examined some basics about assessments and
we've taken a quick look at how our assessments compare to
best practices. Now, let's consider more carefully what
constitutes a high quality, trustworthy assessment.

All assessments are not created equal. Some are better
than others and, just by common sense, we trust some
more than others. Picture an offhand assessment ("That actor
is terrible and surely does not deserve an award
nomination.") delivered by someone we just met at a cocktail
party. Common sense tells us to not place too much credence
in this assessment. Why? For starters, it's only one person's
judgment, the assessor is of unknown qualifications and
expertise, the assessor may be chemically impaired, no
evidence has been offered, and we have no reason for taking
confidence in the process by which the conclusion was
reached. Most of these common sense cautions are
supported by laboratory studies of decision making,
confirming that such conditions lead to lower quality
judgments and decisions.

For a more trusted assessment, picture a financial audit by
one of the major accounting firms. Some high-profile errors

notwithstanding, we can normally place confidence in such assessments because they involve group judgment by trained experts, concrete evidence, and a systematic process based on accepted professional standards. For the same reasons, we can normally take confidence when a panel of expert scientists assesses the quality of a research program, or a team of inspectors assesses the startup readiness of a power plant. These are rigorous assessments by teams of experts with clear criteria and documented evidence.

How, then, can we work toward establishing high quality assessments? Where should we place our efforts?

Three Keys to Quality

Three variables have major impacts on the quality of an assessment and, fortunately, all three are under our control as assessment practitioners. The three determining variables are:

- The Evidence

- The Assessors

- The Assessment Process

These three aspects of an assessment are the best places to focus efforts to achieve higher quality, more trustworthy, assessments.

**FOCAL POINTS FOR
IMPROVING ASSESSMENTS**

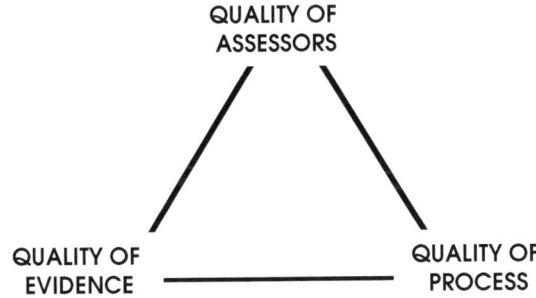

QUALITY OF
ASSESSORS

QUALITY OF
EVIDENCE

QUALITY OF
PROCESS

These three variables are, in principle, independent and unrelated. A given assessment can have good or poor evidence; good or poor assessor(s); a good or poor assessment process, or any mix. In actual practice, however, these variables are correlated with one another, because the practitioners who work to optimize one variable often pay close attention to the other two variables as well.

Part 3

The Evidence

- Types of Evidence

- Quality of Evidence

- Quantitative & Qualitative Evidence

- Document Evidence

- Observational Evidence

- Credibility

Types of Evidence

Evidence varies from documented observations, checklist data and physical measures on carefully developed criteria, as in a professionally conducted safety assessment or power plant readiness assessment, to subjective, descriptive data, as in a wine tasting.

Let's list some of the different types of evidence available and commonly used in assessments. They include:

- Anecdotes and incidents from field observations

- Bibliometric data

- Case study analysis

- Checklist results

- Database searches

- Direct field observations by assessors

- Documents

- Interview responses and quotations

- Measures collected by instruments

- Metrics, scorecards, indicators

- Presentations

- Ratings made by assessors or stakeholders

- Results of market studies, economic analyses

- Scores or observations from exercises (tests, in-baskets, group discussions)

- Subjective reports (taste impressions, etc.)

- Survey responses

- Test scores, essay responses

- Visuals such as blueprints, flow charts

Some assessment evidence is quantitative in nature and some is qualitative. Both are important and we will say more about both types later.

Let's clarify right here one distinction that is sometimes muddled in the literature—the distinction between evidence and data collection tools. For example, a checklist is normally a data collection tool, not evidence. Evidence is the data that result from applying the checklist. Likewise, an exam is a tool; exam scores are evidence. On the other hand, a document or interview quote will usually be evidence. Broadly speaking, if an item was created or brought by the assessors, it is a tool; if it comes from the entity being assessed, it is data or evidence.

Quality of Evidence

"The truth, the whole truth, and nothing but the truth."
–Courtroom Oath

That's what quality assessment evidence is all about—the truth, the whole truth, and nothing but the truth. Strong assessment evidence is objective, directly relates to the characteristic being assessed, fully matches the scope of the assessment, is sufficient in quantity, and is uncontaminated by irrelevant information.

Quality of evidence bears on the accuracy, reliability, and credibility of the whole assessment. The acronym GIGO (garbage in, garbage out) applies in assessments just as it does in information processing. An assessment based on poor evidence cannot be strong, no matter how well everything else is done. The quality of the evidence is foundational to the quality of the assessment, its credibility and, ultimately, the likelihood it will actually be used for something.

So, what is high-quality evidence, and how do we get it? Strong, high-quality evidence has four properties. It is:

- Objective

- Valid

- Sufficient, and

- Pure

Objective

"Based on observable phenomena; presented factually"
                    –Medical Dictionary

Some types of evidence are inherently more objective than others—that is, they reflect external phenomena that can be observed and verified by others. In assessment work, it is uniformly agreed that, while subjective evidence can be very useful, objective evidence is much better. Many of the types of evidence noted earlier (checklist results, database searches, documents, scorecard metrics, etc.) are objective and verifiable. And some types noted earlier are subjective (ratings made by assessors, self reports, etc.). The essential difference is that objective evidence can be verified, examined, and even re-evaluated by others and subjective evidence cannot—it relies on the impressions of persons present at the time and cannot be re-evaluated by others later.

To illustrate, compare bibliometric evidence that might be used in assessing a scientific research program with the evidence from a wine tasting event. Bibliometric data (publications, citations in publications, etc.) are objective statistical counts, verifiable by any outside observer who cares to take the time. In a wine tasting, the evidence is subjective impressions and descriptions given by tasters. Though these impressions might seem objective because they are assigned numerical scores, the raw data are subjective

29

and cannot be inspected by others. Other things being equal, the more objective and verifiable the evidence, the better.

In part, this is because subjective impressions are notoriously influenced by expectations and circumstances. To return to our wine-tasting example:

"In 1963 three researchers secretly added a bit of red food color to a white wine to give it the blush of a rosé. Then they asked a group of experts to rate its sweetness in comparison with the untinted wine. The experts perceived the fake rosé as sweeter than the white, according to their expectation. . . And in a 2008 study a group of volunteers asked to rate five wines rated a bottle labeled $90 higher than another bottle labeled $10, even though the sneaky researchers had filled both bottles with the same wine."
                                                    –L. Mlodinow, 2008

Though subjective data are regarded as inferior, their credibility can be enhanced by adding objective elements to the process—such as increasing the number of assessors and samples. If ten observers all give similar ratings or the same subjective impressions, it adds weight and credibility to the finding. Another way to add credibility is by using recognized, practiced, credentialed experts as observers. The opinions of leading scientists about the merits of a research program are more credible than those of others.

At the outset we noted that one distinguishing characteristic of assessments is that they call for a conclusion or judgment on the part of assessors. Given this inherent subjectivity, the more objective, transparent, and verifiable the evidence on which those judgments are based, the more credibility people usually assign to the assessment.

Valid

When we speak about an individual piece of evidence, validity means how directly and clearly it bears on the characteristic or dimension being assessed—in other words, its relevance. When we speak about the whole package of evidence in an assessment, "validity" means something broader—relevance to be sure, but also sufficiency and purity. Four approaches to establishing relevance are common—Face Validity, Content Validity, Construct Validity, and Criterion Referenced Validity.

Face Validity. Face validity simply means that evidence "on its face" appears to represent the characteristic(s) under study. For example, someone might look at assembly cost-per-unit data and conclude that it is valid evidence in assessing the performance of an assembly line. Or that the number of people fed by a soup kitchen is relevant in assessing the performance of the program.

If evidence does not make sense on the face of it, at the end of the day the assessment will almost surely have credibility

31

problems and be ignored. Though face validity lacks rigor, certain practices can be adopted to add rigor and credibility. One is using known experts to gauge the "face validity" of the evidence. Another is to establish that not just one, but a number of such experts, agree that the evidence is valid on the face of it.

> *If evidence does not make sense on the face of it, the whole assessment is likely to be ignored*

Content Validity. Evidence has Content Validity when it directly represents the characteristic being assessed. As a very simple example, if one is assessing the "deployment of safety devices" and uses a checklist to document safety devices present, one is relying on Content Validity. For another example, some assessment centers demonstrate Content Validity by using exercises drawn directly from work situations.

One tricky point about Content Validity is that the package of evidence must fully and accurately represent the scope of the assessed characteristic and dimensions. To ensure this outcome, the assessment should have a solid, detailed description of the content domain, one that matches the sponsor's understanding of the characteristic being assessed, and use it in specifying the evidence to be collected.

Failure to properly match the content domain of the evidence with the characteristic being assessed can result in disaster. As an example, suppose a jobs training program wants to assess its success in preparing displaced engineers to become science teachers. Suppose a science test is constructed and administered regularly to program graduates, but it is found that far too many graduates, even those with good test scores, are failing on the job. What went wrong?

In this case, suppose an investigation turns up the fact that the test indeed measures all the right science topics, but fails to cover lesson planning, class control, and other skills necessary for success as a teacher. Obviously, the test has only partial content validity.

It's hard to overstate the importance of completely matching the assessment evidence with the meaning and scope of the characteristic being assessed. This point will be referenced again when we cover the topic of Sufficient Evidence.

Construct Validity. Evidence has Construct Validity when it is shown, usually by statistics, to be related to a known, established construct or characteristic. Construct validity is most commonly used when the author of a new test for assessing some human characteristic (e.g., math ability,

33

initiative, depression) claims scores on the new test are valid measures because they correlate with other, established tests of the same characteristic. Reliance on Construct Validity is relatively rare in program, process and organizational assessments.

Criterion Referenced Validity. Evidence has Criterion Referenced Validity when it statistically predicts the criterion variable of interest. For example, if we had the necessary data we could surely show that height is a predictor of success for basketball players. Criterion Referenced Validity is generally regarded as the most scientific and rigorous validation strategy.

Criterion Referenced Validity can be established by comparing assessment outcomes to the current or future success of programs. Such studies should be conducted "in the blind" so the assessment results themselves do not affect outcomes and thereby contaminate the studies.

One of the largest studies of this type was conducted by AT&T and called the Management Progress Study (Bray, Campbell, & Grant, 1974). In this study, the results of assessment centers designed to gauge management abilities were compared to the later management success of participants. Though older, this study remains a landmark among large-scale validations of assessment processes.

More recently, the idea of evidence that reflects program outcomes or consequences is gaining further popularity, especially in education.

"Of critical importance is the concept of evidence based on consequences, a new major validity category in the recently revised Standards." –J. H. McMillan, 2000

Though the term is relatively new, "evidence based on consequences" overlaps significantly with what has traditionally been called Criterion Referenced Validity.

Looking across the various approaches to establishing validity, it is clear that each one tries to do the same thing— demonstrate a direct and unequivocal link between the evidence and the characteristic being assessed. The different validation approaches rely on: 1) common sense; 2) logical argument; and 3) correlation statistics to establish a link.

Sufficient

By sufficient, we mean the package of evidence in an assessment is suitable in completeness, sampling, and depth.

Completeness. As noted earlier in the discussion of Content Validity, assessment evidence must completely cover the stated scope of the assessment. This was illustrated in the example of the job retraining program. For another example, cycle time data would normally be valid evidence in

35

assessing the efficiency of a manufacturing assembly process. But other measures, perhaps work-in-progress, labor time, total cost per assembled unit, etc. could also be valid evidence on efficiency. So cycle time data, if used alone, might be technically valid evidence, just as the test of science knowledge was for the retraining program, but it will not be sufficiently complete to constitute a fully valid package of evidence. It misses the stated scope of the assessment.

> *Mismatching the scope of evidence and the scope of assessment is one of the easiest places to go off the rails*

This sounds simple but is actually where many assessments go off the rails. Without strictly following a rigorous methodology, an assessment team can easily overlook the importance of a proper framework and operational definition for the characteristic(s) they are assessing. For example, assessments often claim to assess the "performance" of a program, focusing their attention on how effective the program is in combating terrorism, preventing the spread of disease, feeding the homeless, or whatever the mission is. In doing so, they equate "effectiveness" with "performance" and ignore other dimensions that most would consider

36

aspects of "performance"—efficiency and, perhaps, sustainability. Some refer to this as "construct underrepresentation." Establishing the right operational definition at the outset always calls for careful, disciplined thought and, oftentimes, consultation with subject matter experts (SME's).

Sampling. Our package of evidence cannot be sufficient if we, for example, take measures from only one assembly line, one product, one time of day, or sample in some other way that does not fully reflect the entity and characteristic we are assessing. When we do so, the data elements in hand may be individually valid (relevant) but, as a package, do not fully represent the stated scope of the assessment. As with the previous examples of incomplete evidence, a poor plan for sampling leads to an incomplete and insufficient package of evidence for the assessment.

Depth of Evidence. A package of evidence that completely, but thinly, covers the scope of an assessment may, likewise, be technically valid (relevant), but insufficient for a high quality assessment. It is a lower quality package of evidence and will result in an assessment that may be valid, but low quality. Imagine the difference between conducting interviews with three people versus thirty on a certain assessment topic. If the interviews are well designed and conducted, the evidence from three is certainly relevant, but

37

the package of evidence collected from thirty persons, though also relevant, would be of much higher quality.

So the question arises, how much evidence is enough? Though it's impossible to give an ironclad formula, there are two rules of thumb which usually apply:

1) In collecting quantitative evidence, the normal rules of statistical operations are a good guide to the minimum amount of data that must be collected. Enough data should be collected that the statistical operations have sufficient power to detect differences and accurately estimate values.

2) When collecting qualitative evidence, one often comes to a point where the data become repetitious; every new bit of evidence repeats something earlier—nothing new and significant is turning up. This point generally marks the earliest possible point for stopping data collection.

Pure

By pure evidence, we mean uncontaminated and unbiased. Perfectly pure evidence is not always available and seldom easy to get, but it is an ideal toward which all professionally conducted assessments strive.

Contamination. In the previous example about assembly line efficiency, our evidence would also be compromised if it included all the proper efficiency variables but also factored in unrelated variables, say employee satisfaction or quality of supervision. Though important issues, these topics are outside the scope of an efficiency assessment. To the degree this unrelated evidence is factored in, it contaminates the evidence package. Sometimes this is referred to as "construct-irrelevant variance."

Though the examples we have chosen here are pretty obvious, in actual practice the issues involving evidence can be quite subtle. It is *always* a useful practice to carefully compare the title and scope of the assessment to the exact nature and scope of the evidence—looking for any lack of full coverage and ensuring that only relevant data are included in each category or dimension assessed.

Bias. Finally, there is the question of bias and how it might contaminate a package of evidence.

"One of the eyebrow-raising statistics about the BPA studies is the stark divergence in results, depending on who funded them. More than 90 percent of the 100-plus government-funded studies performed by independent scientists found health effects from low doses of BPA, while none of the fewer than two dozen chemical-industry-funded studies did."
     –D. Michaels, 2008

We believe deliberate falsification of results is rare in science, but this does not mean that all the evidence we encounter is totally pure and unbiased. Bias creeps into evidence in many ways:

- Small samples
- Selected use of available studies
- Non-publication of unfavorable findings
- Weak competitors chosen as comparatives
- Multiple publication, multiple citings of same data
- Interviews with partisan interviewees

It is not uncommon for unfavorable findings to go unreported, or for studies that find no statistically significant effects to go unpublished. These two tendencies, in addition to the factors listed above, can build bias into the evidence available on an issue. Following is a set of quotes that give the flavor of the debate about evidence bias.

"Smith, Bero and others have catalogued these 'tricks of the trade,' which include testing your drug against a treatment that either does not work or does not work very well; testing your drug against too low or too high a dose of the comparison drug because this will make your drug appear more effective or less toxic; publishing the results of a single trial many times in different forms to make it appear that multiple studies reached the same conclusions; and publishing only those studies, or even parts of studies, that are favorable to your drug, and burying the rest.

Having a financial stake in the outcome changes the way even the most respected scientists approach their research. Scientists make many decisions about the doses, exposure methods and disease definitions they use in their experiments, and each decision affects the result.

For instance, when assessing the risk of exposure to perchlorate, a rocket-fuel ingredient that can affect the thyroid and contaminates many water supplies, scientists on a National Academy of Sciences panel chose perchlorate's effect on thyroid iodine uptake as the most important indicator of its effect on health. On the other hand, scientists working for companies that might have to bear the costs of perchlorate cleanup selected the chemical's effect on one thyroid hormone as the basis of their risk estimation. These scientists estimated a safe level for perchlorate exposure nearly three times higher than that of the NAS scientists.

The answer is de-linking sponsorship and research."
–D. Michaels, 2008

While we are not as quick as some to assign nefarious motives in these situations, we commonly encounter evidence, such as interview quotes, from persons who are not intentionally biased in a particular way, but who hold to

41

reasoned viewpoints based on their experience, their circumstances and the data they know. And we encounter others who hold equally honest, but differing, viewpoints developed in the same way. These views color: 1) how people describe issues; 2) how they interpret situations; 3) what they say to assessors; and, ultimately, 4) the kind of evidence that can flow into an assessment.

> *Assessors must be constantly vigilant in detecting any bias that may be present in the evidence*

Assessors, and especially the assessment leader, must be constantly vigilant in detecting any bias that may be present in the evidence and seek out any balancing evidence that may be available.

Quantitative & Qualitative Evidence

"Precise measures are a good thing, but it's also true that an educated guess about the right variable is worth more than extreme accuracy about the wrong one."
                    –P. Sorenson

All the various types of evidence noted early in this section can be classed as either quantitative or qualitative. Both play important roles as assessment evidence.

Quantitative Evidence

Assessment are often based, at least in part, on evidence that is quantitative and numerical, and such evidence is generally held in high regard. But all numerical evidence is not equal. In 1946, S. S. Stevens set forth a "scale of measures" describing four distinct levels of quantitative measures—Nominal, Ordinal, Interval and Ratio measures.

Nominal Measures simply group data into categories. For example, states, nations and continents are three categories and the names of various states, nations, and continents can be placed as data points in the categories. So a state cannot be in the nation category and vice versa, etc.

43

Assessments apply nominal measurement frequently, when, for example, interview quotes are grouped into topic areas or checklist items into "observed" and "not observed" categories. Sometimes the categories are assigned numbers (i.e., similar to the way products are assigned UPC bar codes), but these numbers are mere labels and no mathematical operations on such labels are legitimate.

Ordinal Measures are very common in assessments and involve scales on which items are ranked relative to one another. Position on an ordinal scale signifies which items are greater or less than others, but not how far apart two items are. We can, for example, say items 1 and 4 on the scale are more distant than items 1 and 3, but that is the limit of what we can say. Anchored rating scales, commonly used in surveys and assessments, are almost always ordinal measures.

As an example, suppose all the agencies in each state are somehow rated as "poor, fair, effective, and very effective" on a scale and we assign the numbers 1, 2, 3, and 4 to the points on the scale. It is a great temptation in such situations, and a very common practice, to then compute an average rating for the agencies in various states and then make comparisons across states. To mathematicians and statistical purists, this practice is completely invalid and nonsensical. Since there is no assurance that the difference between 1 and 2 on such a scale is the same as the difference between 2 and 3, and so forth, we may well be averaging large differences with small ones.

Fortunately, computer modeling studies have shown that misapplying statistics in this way usually does little harm to the conclusions, especially if a fairly large amount of data are involved. This practice is so useful and convenient that it has become commonplace, regardless of its lack of mathematical legitimacy. Practitioners who follow this path should, at a minimum, do so advisedly, and with reasonable efforts to establish equidistant points on their scales.

Interval Measures are similar to ordinal measures except that the points on the scale are equally distant from one another and, therefore, do accurately reflect the distance between items. So the difference between 3 and 4 is the same as the difference between 1 and 2—as it is, for example, on the Farenheit scale of temperature. This allows many mathematically legitimate statistical operations on the data, such as computing means, measures of variability, and so forth. While assessment practitioners should always seek out interval measures, the available evidence often does not have these properties.

45

Ratio Measures also have equal-interval scales, plus the scales have true zero points. This legitimizes additional statistical methods and comparisons.

In assessments, observational evidence (e.g., counting quantities of things) are common ratio measures, and allow one to make ratio and proportion comparisons. For example, they allow saying that Floor 2 has twice as many fire extinguishers as Floor 3 or that Dept Q has one third as many computers per staff person as Dept M, and so forth.

Age, expenses, revenues, market share, errors on tests, etc. are other examples of ratio measures. They are generally the highest and most desirable level of quantitative evidence encountered in assessments.

While criticisms of Stevens' scale of measures have been offered, his conceptualization remains by far the most widely accepted way of looking at quantitative measures.

Qualitative Evidence

"Qualitative methods often aim to produce knowledge of a substantively different kind than other methods."
   –W. Shadish

Most of the qualitative evidence in assessments comes from three kinds of data collection:

• Interviewing

• Direct observation

• Examination of documents

Interviewing. Individual and group interviews generate some of the most compelling evidence in assessments, the best of which is usually a direct quotation. In addition to quotes, the interviewer's impressions and notes can also be useful when a situation must be

---
Individual and group interviews generate some of the most compelling evidence in assessments
---

summarized, though they lack the immediacy and impact of direct quotations.

Some regard it as a best practice for interview questions to be framed in advance and presented the same to each interviewee. Such consistency is a good thing, but

47

experienced interviewers know that rigid interview formats seldom work as well as intended and open-ended questions covering the interviewee's experiences, knowledge, and perceptions are often the most fruitful. Skillful interviewing in assessments is a balancing act that requires: 1) as much consistency in questioning as possible; 2) follow up on discoveries that emerge; 3) a well-tuned "smoke detector;" and 4) discipline in keeping the interview on track. It's not easy.

As noted above, direct quotations add impact to assessment reports, bring credibility and provide readers a more direct experience of the situation. Let us illustrate with sections from a newspaper account of a Humane Society assessment report on a local animal shelter:

"The reply was it is 'not my problem, it's the regular [animal services officer] working the area,' the report states. In another instance . . . the Sweep Team responded that 'it is the tether team's problem, not ours,' the report states.

Before going out on the ride, the observer overheard [a supervisor instructing employees] . . .'That HSUS [expletive] wants to ride with us, so use the new equipment that you were given, watch what you say to him, and make me proud,' the report quotes the supervisor saying."

–Rudolph Bush, 2010

One can readily see that these quotes help paint a picture of operating climate, employee attitudes and sense of responsibility that would be hard to achieve with purely quantitative evidence.

Analyzing qualitative information. As with quantitative data, qualitative information must be analyzed systematically and purposefully. A basic procedure that fits most qualitative data is:

1) Read through all the data.

2) Categorize items (e.g., quotes) by topic or issue.

3) Label the categories according to what fits your assessment.

4) Look for patterns or associations in the data.

5) Count similar items or use other means to establish the relative strength of various issues.

Observational Evidence

Observational evidence comes from field notes, checklists, examination of processes, notes on behaviors, etc. The quality and value of observational data is highest when it is:

- Descriptive and detailed

- Specific, as in checklists

- Objective, verifiable by other observers

In many cases, notations about the context and situation are valuable additions to primary observational data such as checklists, data and notes. Because direct observations lack some of the interpersonal dynamics and unpredictability of interviewing, assessors often find collecting systematic, verifiable evidence by this method easier than by interview.

Document Evidence

Documents, hard copy or electronic, take a great many different forms—ranging from files of reports, business plans, performance measures, policies, records and financial documents to visuals such as blueprints, flow charts and photographs. When assessors examine such documents, the evidence they record is most commonly excerpts from text and descriptions or displays of relevant visuals. The factual nature and verifiability of written documentation make it especially useful and compelling as assessment evidence.

Credibility

The package of evidence in an assessment must be credible for the assessment to be credible. This goes beyond technical validity to include factors that influence the perceptions of sponsors and stakeholders. Objective evidence, multiple observers, multiple sources of information, and specificity in the dimensions and criteria all help bring credibility to an assessment. As we will discuss in the next two sections, the quality of our

> *The credibility of an assessment relies in large part on the credibility of the evidence*

assessors, their training and reputations, and the design and transparency of our assessment process also add to or detract from the credibility of an assessment.

On the negative side, evidence that is inherently subjective tends to reduce credibility. Even among wine critics, the subjective and unreliable nature of the evidence in a wine tasting, though controlled as well as possible, means it must be regarded with some measure of skepticism.

The bottom line is that the credibility of an assessment relies in large part on the credibility of the evidence, the manner in which it is presented, and the degree to which the dimensions, criteria and process used in the assessment make sense to readers.

SUMMARY OF EVIDENCE QUALITY

DESIRABLE	LESS DESIRABLE
Objective, Verifiable	Subjective, Cannot Verify
Valid, Relevant	Irrelevant Items Included
Quantitative, Ratio Scale	Categorical or Ordinal Data
Sufficient, Complete	Thin or Partially Sampled
Pure	Contaminated or Biased

Part 4

The Assessors

- Four Key Roles

- Quality Assessors

- Selection

- Training

- Management

- Bias and Politics

Four Key Roles

In every assessment, multiple roles and tasks must be fulfilled. Often a team is assembled to fill these roles; other times the roles may be collapsed such that one individual fills several roles.

We identify four roles in every assessment:

1) **Sponsor.** Every assessment is sponsored by some person or organization. In the case of self-assessments, the sponsor is the assessed entity or its leaders. In external assessments, the sponsor might be a funding organization, customer, regulator, oversight agency, or other stakeholder concerned with the entity and the characteristic to be assessed.

2) **Assessment Leader or Facilitator.** The best assessment leaders bring three attributes:

- Expertise in the assessment process

- Leadership in managing the assessor team

- Reputation for fairness and lack of bias

These are essential attributes. To the degree they are absent, the resulting assessment will suffer in quality, reliability and credibility. If these qualities are not sufficiently present in the available leaders, the assessment should be postponed or a suitable workaround employed.

3) **Assessors.** The best assessors bring four attributes:

- Knowledge of assessment subject matter

- Trained

- Unbiased

- Independent

4) **Assistants.** In large assessments, assistants sometimes help with data collection, analysis, and other tasks. It is preferable for assessors to personally do this work, as there is no substitute for first-hand familiarity with the evidence in an assessment. Where assistants are involved, the ideal characteristics of assessors noted above apply to them as well. Allowances can be made in cases where assistants' tasks are narrowly defined, more clerical in nature, and/or do not call for interpretation of data.

Quality Assessors

"Since assessment is a judgmental process, the quality of the judge is of great importance." –J. Moses

Because the quality and capabilities of the assessors are so crucial to the ultimate quality of the assessment, let us expand on their qualifications. Ideally, each assessor will have appropriate familiarity with the type of entity being assessed (e.g., nuclear power plants, graduate education, state agencies, manufacturing processes, research programs) and with the characteristic being assessed (e.g., performance, risk, readiness, strategy, efficiency). Each assessor should be selected carefully and trained as necessary in performing his or her role. Each should likewise be fair-minded, unbiased, able to see beyond his or her own professional views, willing to do the work of first-hand data collection, and independent of any compromising financial, social, or other connections to the assessed entity.

"Therefore, participants in performance-based assessments must be technically competent in the areas they are assessing. For example, if an assessor is evaluating a welding process, the assessor relies heavily on his or her knowledge of welding codes, welding processes, and metallurgy, rather than just verifying simple procedure compliance."
–EFCOG, 2004

"EPA should always make every effort to use peer reviewers who do not have any conflict of interest or an appearance of a lack of impartiality, and who are completely independent."
–EPA, 2006

57

Selection

Some organizations with ongoing assessment programs, such as the National Labs, have detailed criteria and requirements for assessment leaders and for assessment team members. In those with which we are familiar, background is checked by examining the potential assessor's *curriculum vitae* and a rating form is used to assign point values for each of the following qualifications:

- Independence—unbiased and without present or previous ties to the area being assessed

- Education—points assigned by degree

- Experience—points assigned for technical expertise and experience with the characteristics to be assessed

- Certifications—points assigned for professional, association, and governmental affiliations and certifications

- Performance—points assigned for previous work performance

- Training—points assigned for assessment courses completed

- Experience—points assigned for previous assessment experience

- Communication Skills—points assigned for writing and verbal skills

In this system, assessors must qualify with a certain number of points before being considered for an assessment team and, in addition, must pass managerial review and approval. As one of the more thorough approaches to selecting members of an assessment team, this approach can offer to others a positive model of rigor and professionalism.

For another example, consider the selection process used in jury trials. Even in misdemeanor cases, attorneys use the *voir dire* process, questioning potential jurors about their attitudes with regard to the law involved in a case, and whether their personal and professional experience, attitudes, and beliefs might unduly affect how they examine evidence and render a verdict. The seriousness and importance of this matter is reflected in the fact that courts sometimes devote nearly as much time to the *voir dire* process as to the evidence and arguments of a case.

Across the board, assessments show great variation in the amount of attention paid to assessor qualifications. Since this matter bears so directly on the quality of the assessment and its trustworthiness with the sponsor and others, we believe it is difficult to overemphasize the importance of carefully selecting the best assessors.

Training

We noted earlier that assessors must be knowledgeable about the entity being assessed and the characteristic being assessed, as well as able to perform their tasks in an unbiased way. This calls for a well-organized briefing session for the assessors and, depending on their previous experience, a training session. These events must be sufficiently thorough that each assessor has a solid understanding of:

- The entity and characteristic to be assessed.

- The assessor's role in collecting and analyzing evidence.

- The assessor's responsibility in presenting and judging evidence.

- The sources of bias and contamination in assessments.

- The do's and don'ts necessary to avoid contaminating the evidence or the judgments of others.

- How to record evidence consistently.

- How to judge evidence and use any rating tools involved.

Leadership

In the best assessments, assessors are guided throughout by the assessment leader or facilitator. This person ensures that each assessor:

- Is properly selected

- Is properly trained

- Knows his/her tasks and performs them in a timely and diligent way

- Performs according to the assessment plan and avoids contaminating the process by discussing evidence out of turn, using force of personality, power or position rather than evidence to convince others.

Bias and Politics

"One person's truth is another person's bias; are these honest differences in judgment, the influence of local culture, or just plain politics?" –J. Thoresen

"Individuals with a conflict of interest in particular areas generally should not participate as reviewers in those areas of the peer review." –DOE EERE Peer Review Guide, 2004

Assessors in Contested Situations. Many assessments, while they claim to be impartial proceedings, are conducted in situations heavy with adversarial overtones. Even scientific peer reviews too often fall into this category. In such situations, the adversaries will often do their best to influence the outcomes of the assessments—typically working for or against the involvement of particular assessors, sponsoring studies that generate favorable evidence, filing lawsuits, and otherwise trying to influence the assessment.

Without taking sides on the issue itself, let us offer, as a good example, the controversy surrounding assessment of the health effects of Bisphenol A (BPA), a chemical used in hardening polycarbonate plastics and epoxy resins. The stakeholders in this particular example are the Environmental Protection Agency, chemical industry groups, environmental advocates, health advocates, and the glass industry.

As in many scientific assessments, only a few leading experts are qualified to sit on a panel assessing the research and safety of BPA. Most of these experts are aligned with one or another of the stakeholders in the controversy, either as employees, grant recipients, active environmentalists or health advocates. The tenor of the arguments in this case can be illustrated by a few quotations:

"When the government removes top scientists from positions because they express concerns over potential health risks from industrial chemicals—at the same time leaving dozens of scientists with direct ties to the chemical industry on review panels—something is very wrong."
                                                    –Houlihan, 2008

"In fact, experts with a stake in the outcome—and therefore an appearance of conflict—may be some of the most knowledgeable and up-to-date experts because they have concrete reasons to maintain their expertise."
                                                    –EPA, 2006

"The Center for Science in the Public Interest, which campaigns on health and food safety issues, believes that EPA's action violates the US Federal Advisory Committee Act. The law requires that panels be fairly balanced in terms of their viewpoints and that any final report be the result of independent judgment."
                                                    –Trager, 2008

"The chairperson's pre-existing bias advocating the ban of deca-BDE is not consistent with the scientific standards of an independent peer review."
                                                    –Harrington, (n.d.)

"EPA is also defending its actions. Tim Lyons, the agency's deputy press secretary, said EPA's peer review guidelines specify that potential committee members can be considered conflicted if they previously made public statements indicating a particular position on the topic under consideration.

63

The Environmental Working Group (EWG), which obtained the letters through a Freedom of Information request, says that industry is taking aim at the handful of public service scientists who effectively counterbalance corporate interests on EPA safety assessment panels."
                                                    –Trager, 2008

"In order to maintain the integrity of peer review for agency decisions, EPA must:

- *Collect information regarding all current and past financial ties between prospective panelists and companies who might benefit from weakened safety standards;*

- *Create formal, public records of their determination of bias for each scientist selected as reviewer; and*

- *Release all records of any similar instances in which EPA has removed panel members or published altered versions of EPA expert reviewer submissions."*
                                            –Lunder & Houlihan, 2008

Even from a distance, we can see the difficulty of selecting assessors and conducting fair, objective assessments in such circumstances. Some experts (Cronbach et al., 1980) have suggested that assessments, especially those involving public policy, are essentially political activities and serve to help govern various social programs. Assessment leaders, sponsors and assessors must recognize the fact that evaluations in these situations will be subject to many political forces and have repercussions that greatly affect stakeholders.

64

How can useful, reasonably valid, assessments be conducted in adversarial situations?

- First, by engaging as many truly impartial assessors as possible.

- Second, if potentially-biased assessors must be used, by ensuring that they equally represent the opposing factions.

- Third, by ensuring a strong, impartial leader controls the assessment process, and

- Fourth, by recognizing that the normal assessment process for peer reviews will likely have to be modified for these situations.

These situations call for a process of analyzing, presenting and judging evidence that is suitable to an adversarial proceeding—a process patterned after congressional hearings, jury trials, debates or other methods that allow for conflicting sets of evidence to be presented and rebutted in a structured, orderly manner.

"Incorporation of these opposing views within a single evaluation reflects a conscious effort to assume fairness and balance and illuminate both strengths and weaknesses of the program." —Worthen, 1990

The ordinary process for scientific peer reviews is especially troubling when Federal agencies determine the composition of the panels and they, themselves, are responsive to different philosophies depending on the political party in office. An assessment method designed specifically for adversarial situations is clearly more appropriate than letting outcomes be overly influenced by outside forces.

Conclusion. When we summarize the desirable qualifications for assessors, as in the table below, they seem to reflect common sense. But many high-profile assessments, like the BPA case, are accused of not meeting these standards.

The degree to which these qualifications are fulfilled determines, in large part, the confidence we can place in the resulting assessment. Though compromises must often be made, there is little disagreement on the assessor qualities which support the best assessments.

SUMMARY OF ASSESSOR QUALITY

DESIRABLE	LESS DESIRABLE
Team of Assessors	Single Assessor
Trained and Practiced	Untrained, Unpracticed
Knowledgeable of Entity	No Knowledge of Entity
Understands Characteristic	New to Characteristic
Recognized as Unbiased	Strong Opinions on Topic
No Ties to Entity	Compromising Ties

Part 5

The Process

- Introduction

- Criteria

- Separation of Stages

- Avoiding Contamination

- Tools and Models

- Lessons Learned

- A Process Model

Introduction

"Multiple observers, multiple sources of information, and specifically defined objective dimensions of performance all add to the objectivity of the process."   –J. Moses

In addition to the quality of evidence and quality of assessors, the quality of the assessment process itself bears on the quality and trustworthiness of an assessment. Earlier, we noted the importance of designing special assessment processes for adversarial circumstances. Here we will focus on the standard process for non-adversarial situations, though many of the same principles apply to both.

All assessment processes, normal and adversarial, involve a number of steps and stages. Their design can contribute to a reliable, valid assessment or to a low-quality, contaminated assessment. An optimal assessment process involves, at minimum:

- Clear Criteria

- Separation of Stages

- Lack of Contamination

- Effective Use of Tools and Models

- Lessons Learned

We will consider these principles and how they influence the assessment, and then diagram a general model for the assessment process.

Criteria

"There's no sense in being precise when you don't even know what you are talking about." –J. von Neumann

The better specified your assessment criteria, and the less need for interpretation, the clearer your assessment tasks and outcomes will be. This means explicitly specifying, in advance, the characteristics and dimensions to be assessed. It also means defining the standards that distinguish between levels on each characteristic or dimension and, in addition, the evidence and sources of evidence that will be used to distinguish between the levels.

The development of strong criteria begins with the requests and requirements of the sponsor. These provide a foundation, but seldom adequately operationalize exactly what will be assessed. The assessment team, guided by the assessment leader, must apply its professional know-how to establish the operational definition of exactly what will be assessed and develop a clear set of criteria and standards for the levels of each characteristic. These normally should be reviewed with the sponsor, refined if necessary, and signed-off before work begins. As this part of the process unfolds, four points provide guidance:

1) Sources of criteria include professional experience, other assessments, professional standards, engineering standards, political/acceptability criteria, stakeholder priorities, oversight requirements, rules and regulations, etc.

2) The more tangible and observable the evidence in relation to the standard, the less judgment is required at the time of data collection and the more reliable the assessment.

3) The more binary the observational data, the more reliable the assessment (e.g., checklists of "present/absent" for observations).

4) The more anchoring present in any rating scales, the more reliable and valid the instrument and the assessment.

Separation of Stages

The separation-of-stages principle is simple and linear—criteria before evidence before evaluation.

CRITERIA → EVIDENCE → EVALUATION

As noted above, criteria for the assessment must be nailed down at the outset, before any data collection or analysis. Criteria developed in advance help determine exactly what evidence will be required, the size of the task ahead, and what data collection tools must be designed.

> *Criteria developed in advance help determine exactly what evidence will be required*

As in a courtroom, all the evidence must be "on the table" before assessors begin the final evaluation. The design of the assessment, training of assessors, and supervision by the facilitator should all work toward averting any premature evaluations. Before the evaluation stage, assessor activities should be limited to collecting evidence and organizing it according to the issues on which it bears. The guiding principle is that all evidence relevant to a specific characteristic or dimension should be held in mind as assessors *begin* making judgments on that characteristic or dimension.

71

Avoiding Contamination

One important function served by a carefully-structured assessment process is the avoidance of cross-contamination. Assessment processes that do not specifically guard against cross-contamination—of activities, assessors and evaluations—result in less reliable and credible assessments than those that do.

Contamination across Activities. The activities of criteria development, evidence collection, and evaluation should be sequentially separate with no overlap. Premature evidence collection can contaminate the development of criteria, and premature evaluation can contaminate how the remaining evidence is collected and perceived.

The possibility of cross-contamination between data collection and evaluation is a risk that is accepted when assessors use scoring rubrics or evaluation matrices to judge evidence in real time—while it is being observed. When scoring objective, observable evidence (e.g., presence or absence of fire extinguishers) this risk is acceptably low, but it becomes much higher when the evidence requires more interpretation (e.g., a scientific peer review). When assessors draw conclusions on early bits of evidence, it can easily affect how subsequent bits of evidence are perceived and evaluated—a clear case of contamination. It is a much sounder practice for assessors to merely record and categorize evidence, making no judgments until the evaluation session begins.

Contamination across Assessors. Assessments are often team activities. If some assessors unduly influence others on the team (by personality, status, or other irrelevant variables) in the course of criteria development, data collection or, especially, during evaluation, the value of a team approach is severely reduced. Careful design of the evaluation session plus strong monitoring by the assessment leader are among the best controls for these contaminating influences. The benefit of multiple assessors is greatest when each makes independent judgments and contributes an independent perspective to the effort.

> *Careful design of
> the evaluation session
> plus strong monitoring
> by the leader are among
> the best ways to control
> contaminating influences*

Contamination across Evaluations. One metaphor for the assessment process is that of a river and tributaries. Think of the final evidence-based evaluation in which assessors reach consensus as the river; with tributaries representing the separate work of the assessors in collecting, analyzing and categorizing various lines of evidence. Though imperfect, the river metaphor fixes a useful mental picture of the

73

separateness of streams of evidence and work of individual assessors.

The assessment process is compromised if assessors collaborate on evaluations before the final session, or if they allow the evidence on one characteristic or dimension to affect favorably (the so-called "halo effect") or unfavorably (the "horns effect") how another dimension is viewed. Again, monitoring by the assessment leader and careful design of data presentation during the evaluation phase can help control such effects.

The goal is for the assessment process to keep, to the degree possible, each assessor's analysis and evaluations uninfluenced by other assessors, other evidence, and other dimensions until they have been independently thought out.

Tools & Models

The appropriate use of tools and models makes an important contribution to the quality of an assessment process. There are at least three categories of tools and models—those helpful in: 1) planning the assessment; 2) defining characteristics and criteria; and 3) making evaluations and ratings. Since reviewing even a sample of these tools and models takes considerable space, they have been given separate treatment in Part 7.

Lessons Learned

Collecting and documenting the practices that contributed to the success of an assessment and, in particular, those that didn't, is the final step in a high-quality assessment process. Some organizations apply very specific and formal methods for collecting this information. Where such methods are not in place, even an informal final meeting to collect information and viewpoints can be highly beneficial in designing the next assessment. Ensuring that this happens is another responsibility that rests with the Assessment Leader.

Collecting Lessons Learned feeds your continuous improvement cycle and facilitates steady, incremental improvements in your assessment processes. We will have more to say about continuous improvement in Part 8.

A Process Model

The figure below outlines a general model for the assessment process. We believe it allows for incorporating all the desirable features discussed here and in other chapters.

This model was drawn with the assessment of entities such as programs, processes, agencies and institutions in mind. But it applies, we believe, very well to every other possible type of assessment.

ASSESSMENT PROCESS MODEL

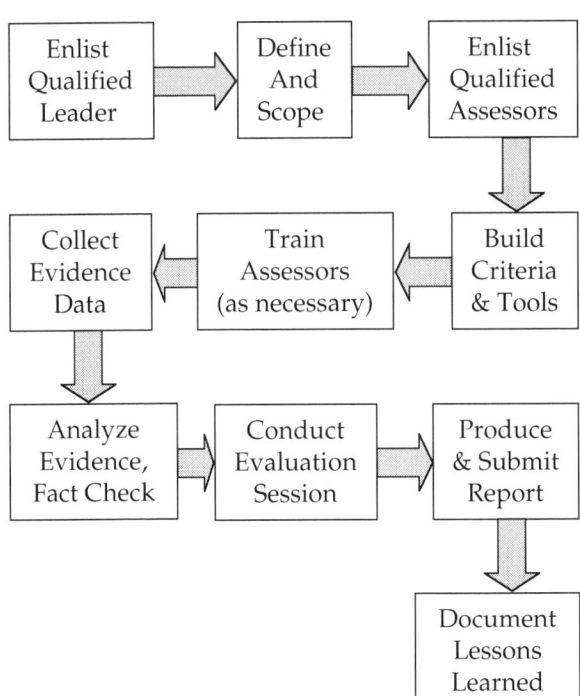

The features we have noted here are hallmarks of the best processes for conducting assessments. Optimizing all of them simultaneously can be a daunting task, and is seldom achieved. But that is the ideal, and the challenge, of designing the best possible assessment process.

SUMMARY OF PROCESS QUALITY

DESIRABLE	LESS DESIRABLE
Clear Criteria at Outset	Vague Criteria
Separation of Activities	Cross-Contaminated Activities
Independent Assessors	Cross-Contaminated Assessors
Separation of Evaluations	Cross-Contaminated Evaluations
Orderly, Managed Process	Weak Leader, Disorder
Supporting Tools, Models	Relevant Concepts Ignored
Lessons Learned	No Evaluation of the Process

Part 6

Assessment Principles & Best Practices

- Lessons from the Courtroom

- 22 Principles and Practices

Lessons from the Courtroom

In the Introduction, we promised an eclectic approach, looking for best practices that might be applied more widely across assessments. Before we enumerate those principles and practices, let's examine some from a special type of assessment familiar to all of us—the jury trial. Jury trials embody a number of good practices that could apply to all types of assessments:

1) **Strong Leader.** Judges have the responsibility and authority to maintain an orderly process that follows prescribed steps and rules.

2) **Multiple Assessors.** A panel of jurors offers the same advantage as a panel of assessors—better accuracy and less chance of error.

3) **Unbiased Assessors.** Jurors are subjected to careful questioning by prosecution and defense attorneys (*voir dire*) to uncover biases that might disqualify them.

4) **Balanced Advocacy.** Both sides are represented by attorneys presenting evidence and acting as advocates.

5) **Assessor Training.** While their training is minimal, jurors do receive a briefing from the judge on their deliberations and the points of law at issue.

6) **Quality Evidence.** Rules of evidence exist and are enforced to ensure relevance, materiality, verifiability, etc. Both sides are allotted specific periods for presenting evidence and for cross examination to improve the quality of evidence.

7) **No Premature Conclusions.** All the evidence is on the table, presented and argued, before jurors begin deliberating.

Some of these practices address the quality of assessors, some the quality of evidence, and some the quality of the assessment process.

For all their good qualities, jury trials are not perfect assessments. For example, the assessors—jurors—could be better trained, more knowledgeable about the trial process, and more practiced in evaluating evidence. But jury trials are not intended to be optimal assessment processes. Rather, they seek an optimal balance of the practical requirements, the practices that lead to good assessments, and the practices that protect the rights of defendants.

81

22 Principles & Practices

Now, let us briefly enumerate the principles and best practices we find across the assessment literature. While each of these applies to every type of assessment, some are more practical in a given situation, and some less practical. Many of these principles and best practices are obvious from common sense, but they are met in varying degrees, and often not at all, in everyday assessments.

Here are the principles and practices we have already touched on in previous sections. The best assessments have:

1. Stated purpose and goal

2. Clear criteria and scales of evaluation

3. Respected, qualified leader

4. Multiple assessors

5. Independent assessors

6. Qualified, trained assessors

7. Clear criteria, determined before evidence

8. Objective, verifiable evidence

9. Valid evidence

10. Lack of contamination

11. Controlled, managed evaluation process

12. Active efforts to avert and mitigate bias

13. Separate, independent judgments by assessors

14. Lessons Learned Reviews

Now let's enumerate some additional principles and best practices that we have not yet discussed. The best assessments involve:

15. **Consultation.** The sponsor and other stakeholders are consulted in the assessment design. In some cases, the evidence, once collected, is reviewed with entity stakeholders to ensure accuracy and acceptance later.

16. **Multiple methods.** Multiple types of evidence and multiple methods of collecting evidence are used whenever appropriate, with each method contributing to a rich, credible package of evidence.

17. **Efforts to ensure usage.** Stakeholder needs for information, stakeholder deadlines, and effective reporting mechanisms are incorporated to optimize the acceptance, understanding, and use of the assessment.

18. **Control of extraneous variables.** Assessment design and tools minimize the effects of irrelevant variables, such as cultural differences and individual skill differences.

19. **Independence.** While they consult with stakeholders, the assessment team retains full control of the design, execution, and reporting of the assessment.

83

20. **Holistic participation by assessors.** The assessment of each characteristic or dimension is the product of the whole team. In assessing a facility, for example, assessors are not assigned to separately evaluate safety, security, quality of management, environmental impact, etc. Partitioning forfeits the benefit of a team assessment.

21. **Feedback and improvement.** Assessments, especially those to improve performance, should be coupled with feedback, goal setting and action. While this is common sense, assessments are routinely conducted that result in no serious attention to improvement by organizational leaders.

22. **Efficiency and practicality.** Efficiency and practicality are widely cited as good practices in assessment. For example, assessments that go beyond "smile-sheet surveys" to thoroughly assess the outcomes of training programs can easily cost more than the programs themselves. The question for the assessment becomes: How can best practices be maximized in a valid, useful assessment that is affordable?

Part 7

Useful Tools & Models

- Introduction

- Planning Aids

- Design Aids

- Evaluation Aids

Introduction

Earlier we noted that tools and models can strengthen the process of assessment, though the topic was too lengthy to engage at that time. Now the time has come to review a selected sample of tools and models that can enhance assessment tasks. Some are useful in planning the assessment, some in designing the characteristics and dimensions to be assessed, and some in the evaluation stage where evidence and judgment meet.

Planning Aids

As with any complex effort, assessments benefit from good planning. The assessment literature offers several planning aids, though most are too sketchy, or too devoted to one type of assessment, to be broadly useful. But there are exceptions.

Stufflebeam Checklists. One exception is a set of checklists for planning and conducting assessments published by Stufflebeam (1999, 2002, 2004). While these will fit some assessments better than others, they do cover issues that should be important reminders to all assessment planners. For example, one of the checklists (Stufflebeam, 2002) covers activities involved in:

1) Assessment contracts

2) Assesssment context evaluation

3) Input evaluation

4) Process evaluation

5) Impact evaluation

6) Effectiveness evaluation

7) Sustainability evaluation

8) Transportability evaluation

9) Metaevaluation, and

10) Final report

The Department of Energy (DOE) Checklist. Another exception is the "Manager's Checklist for Conducting a Peer Review" (Department of Energy EERE Peer Review Guide, 2004, p. 66), one of several useful appendices in the DOE Guide. These appendices contain many items that apply to all assessments. Here is the Manager's Checklist:

1) Peer review leadership

2) Scope, purpose, and evaluation criteria

3) Cost and logistics

4) Selection of reviewers

5) Evaluation guidelines and tools

6) On-site conduct of review

7) Report and other post-review activities

8) Examples of review questions

9) Peer review timeline

10) Reviewer expertise

11) Conflict of interest

12) Nondisclosure agreements

13) Guidelines for reviewers and chairpersons

14) Evidence materials

15) Program evaluation rating forms

16) Review evaluation instrument

The Conducting Assessments Process Model. A final tool that may be useful to those planning an assessment is the General Assessment Process noted in this book. This model was diagrammed earlier and will be outlined in more detail in Part 8. The model has six main categories of activities, with a group of step-by-step items in each category. The main categories are:

1) Initial preparation

2) Planning and design

3) Collecting evidence

4) Analysis and evaluation

5) Report

6) Continuous improvement

Design Aids

The scope and focus of an assessment is established early in the process, beginning with the entity to be assessed and the particular characteristic of that entity to be assessed. When a single, broad characteristic is to be assessed (e.g., Performance, Quality, Readiness, Safety) it is often desirable to operationalize the characteristic as a set of specific dimensions to be evaluated. For example, a safety assessment might be parceled into such dimensions as incidents, signage, response readiness, and so forth. We can only assess a broad characteristic after we specify exactly what that characteristic means.

How do assessment designers determine the specific dimensions for a complex characteristic? Here are several methods in everyday use:

Facilitator-led teams. Many times, the assessment leader will convene a group to determine the operational definitions of the characteristic being assessed. These teams are comprised of subject matter experts, persons representing the entity being assessed, the assessors, or a mix of the three. The quality of the dimensions produced by such a team will depend on the expertise of those involved, their knowledge of best practices, any benchmarking and research that has been completed, etc. While this method is the one most adaptable to a new, specific situation, it is also perhaps the most variable in quality.

Oversight requirements. The requirements and interests of oversight agencies and other assessment sponsors commonly dictate many of the characteristics and dimensions to be assessed. In some cases (e. g., the National Laboratories, various nonprofits) the content and frequency of certain assessments are part of the organization's performance contract with its funders.

Professional and regulatory standards. In many types of assessments, collections of professional standards (such as the Generally Accepted Accounting Principles in finance, published standards in materials handling, published standards in toxic waste disposal, etc.) furnish dimensions that further delineate the characteristic being assessed.

Model-guided approaches. In other cases, a theory, model, or well-developed construct helps guide the development of dimensions for an assessment. There are many such models. Since many assessments are conducted with a focus on the "performance" of a program, agency, or organization, let's explore the meaning of this term and how certain popular models can help us better understand and operationalize it as a set of dimensions.

Models for "performance"

Program Logic Model. The Program Logic Model (also called simply Logic Model) is a useful, versatile, and widely-cited model for characterizing a program or agency. To summarize the big picture of an entire program or organization, a Logic Model outlines the Inputs, Activities, Outputs and Outcomes.

What does a Logic Model look like? Here's an example we have shown elsewhere (Frost, 2007) that summarizes a not-for-profit children's chorus:

Logic Model—Children's Choral Society

Inputs	Activities	Outputs	Outcomes
Resources: *Human* --Staff: (#) *Financial* --Tuition ($) --Performances ($) --Contributions ($) *Facilities* --Performance hall --Rehearsal space --Office space *Technologies* --Ticketing system --Attendance tracking --Donor database --Music library *Measures:*	*Programs & Services:* --Choruses (#) --Rehearsals (#) --Performances (#) --Regional Tours --National Tours --School Concerts --Summer Camp *Measures:*	*Learning:* --Musical literacy --Voice technique --Discipline --Diversity --Quality music *Community:* --Support for music --Chorale enrollment --Patron attendance --City ambassadors *Measures:*	*Condition:* --Changed lives --Musical careers --Civic mindedness --Community image *Measures:*

A Logic Model would suggest we look to dimensions of Inputs, Activities, Outputs and Outcomes in assessing the performance of a program, agency, or organization. Prior to the use of Logic Models, assessments of programs and agencies often overemphasized activities and outputs. Assessments were focused on clients served, training provided, inmates housed, etc. Logic Models have rightly put "outcomes" into the equation, suggesting that programs and agencies must also be judged on the ultimate outcomes they were designed to bring forth (e.g., changed lives, employee safety, lower crime rates).

So Logic Models can be helpful guides in specifying relevant dimensions for assessing performance. With the widespread use of Logic Models, there has developed some tendency to think of performance primarily in terms of Outputs and Outcomes. To illustrate how important, and sometimes tricky, it can be to design the proper set of dimensions for assessing a complex characteristic, let's consider what some alternative models have to say about "performance."

Enterprise Performance Model. The Enterprise Performance Model (Frost, 2007) is another guide we might use in defining "performance" and choosing dimensions for an assessment. This model suggests there are three overarching dimensions to performance.

ENTERPRISE PERFORMANCE MODEL

This model suggests Effectiveness, Efficiency, and Sustainability as dimensions for defining and assessing the

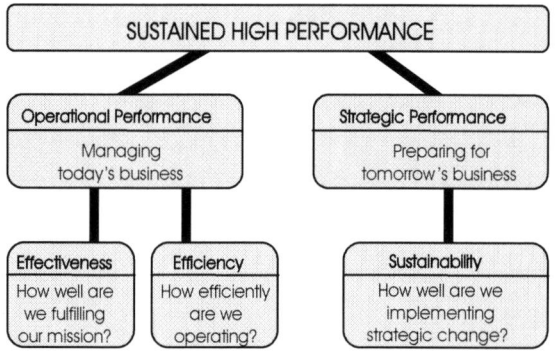

performance of a program, agency, or organization. The evidence for Effectiveness might turn out to be similar to the evidence for Outputs and Outcomes under the Program Logic Model. Likewise, the Efficiency dimension might overlap somewhat with the Inputs and Activities dimensions of that model. But the Sustainability dimension suggested by the Enterprise Performance Model would lead to a whole new category of evidence on "performance" not normally suggested by the Program Logic Model, that on Implementing Strategic Change.

Balanced Scorecard Model. The Balanced Scorecard (Kaplan & Norton, 1992) is a third model for defining performance and setting assessment dimensions, one that has been very popular in business organizations and, to a lesser degree, in nonprofit and government organizations. It asserts that there are four perspectives or dimensions to organizational performance—the Financial, Internal Processes, Learning and Growth, and Customer perspectives.

BALANCED SCORECARD MODEL

Though the Balanced Scorecard overlaps with the other two models we've covered, it is more business flavored and slightly more specific, leading to four somewhat different dimensions for performance. Especially in cases where the entity to be assessed already makes use of the Balanced Scorecard, an assessment team might do well to follow these four dimensions.

95

One can readily see how these three models might help assessors operationally define a broad characteristic like performance. An even more challenging situation arises when a sponsor requests an assessment of an entire organization or agency, without specifying a characteristic like "performance" to be assessed. Models are available to help with such a task and we will review three of them next. In such a situation, the assessment leader and assessment team will need to outline a set of characteristics and dimensions based on an appropriate model and their professional judgment, then gain consensus with the assessment sponsor and other stakeholders.

Baldrige Award Categories. The categories used in Baldrige Award examinations (National Institute of Standards and Technology, 2011) offer dimensions that might well be used in other broad-gauge assessments of agencies, institutions, or organizations. They are:

- Leadership

- Strategic Planning

- Customer Focus

- Measurement, Analysis, and Knowledge Management

- Workforce Focus

- Operations Focus

- Results

The Program Assessment Rating Tool (PART). The Program Assessment Rating Tool (Office of Management and Budget, 2003-2008) is a device used for several years in assessing programs of the Federal Government. Its stated goals are to drive improvements in program performance and inform budget decisions; it is described as a consistent way to assess effectiveness across Federal programs. We might note, in light of the previous discussion, that while the stated goal is to "improve performance," the tool nominally targets only one dimension of performance—effectiveness. PART supports the review of program design, program implementation, and program results, using a questionnaire tool divided into four sections:

1) Program Purpose and Design

2) Strategic Planning

3) Program Management

4) Program Results

In using this tool, points were assigned to the answers on questionnaire items, from which an overall program rating was developed—with programs described as Effective, Moderately Effective, Adequate, Ineffective, or Results Not Demonstrated.

The Office of Management and Budget has applied this rating system to a large number of Federal programs and   97 published the results as part of its annual budgeting process, beginning in 2003 with 234 programs and expanding beyond that in subsequent years. PART is yet another model that might guide the setting of dimensions in a broad-gauge agency or organizational assessment.

CIPP Model. The CIPP Evaluation Model (Stufflebeam, 2003) is described as "a comprehensive framework for guiding evaluations of programs, projects, products, institutions, and systems." CIPP stands for Context evaluation, Input evaluation, Process evaluation, and Product evaluation.

This model was originally developed by Stufflebeam in the 1960's and has been particularly popular in education. It is based on a simple process model involving inputs, process, and outputs and was, at least in concept, a forerunner of the Program Logic Model. The basic CIPP model suggests program assessment must strive to answer four questions and four sub-questions:

1) **Context** What needs were addressed?

2) **Input** Are the right resources and plans applied?

3) **Process** Were the plans carried out?

4) **Product** Did the project or program succeed?

    a) **Impact**—Was right group impacted?

    b) **Effectiveness**—Were key needs met?

c) **Sustainability**—Will success continue?

d) **Transportability**—Can the program be used elsewhere?

The CIPP Model has provided guidance in defining the dimensions for many assessments over the years.

Conclusion. We readily admit the models shown here are a narrow representation of those that might serve as guides in defining assessment dimensions. We trust they illustrate how an appropriate model can be used in operationalizing the characteristic being assessed, as well as help build stakeholder understanding and establish credibility for the assessment.

In the end, a valid assessment is one that gauges what it says it gauges. And models help establish this congruity. It's fine if we set out to assess effectiveness, define it appropriately,

> *Properly matching evidence*
> *to assessed characteristics*
> *is vital to the validity*
> *of an assessment*

and proceed to conduct the assessment. But there is something amiss when we set out to assess performance and our evidence covers only effectiveness. We have underrepresented the construct, just as if we intended to assess climate and used only evidence on rainfall. So, properly matching evidence to assessed characteristics and dimensions is vital to the validity, and the credibility, of an assessment. When we operationalize the characteristic to be assessed, we are defining in a concrete way exactly what we are assessing, and shaping the types of evidence that will be relevant.

Whether it's performance, weather, operational readiness or something else we are assessing, merely specifying the characteristic to be assessed suddenly obliges us to deal with certain models, definitions and constructs that have already staked out claims to the meaning of the term we are borrowing. We must make choices when we operationalize the characteristics we are assessing, and we must take account of how others have described the territory if we want our assessments to be credible.

Evaluation Aids

In addition to those useful in the planning and design phases, there are also models and tools for the evaluation phase. We will outline a few of the more important ones as illustrations.

From Evidence to Evaluation. After all the evidence is collected, assessors must turn to the task of organizing, analyzing, and applying it toward an evaluation. One of the most useful tools for this task is the ubiquitous anchored rating scale and its variants—rubrics and maturity ladders.

Anchored Rating Scales. Anchored rating scales do not apply in every circumstance, but overall they are one of the most widely used tools for making ratings, for collecting evidence, and for summarizing conclusions.

For many years now, people have been asked to assign a number (say from 1 to 5, 1 to 10, or 1 to 100) to reflect the quantity or extent of some characteristic. Or, in the case of a continuous rating scale, they might be asked to place a mark on a line somewhere between two end points.

It was quickly discovered in these efforts that rating scales which were "anchored" with descriptive phrases at the ends, and at intermediate points, yielded more reliable results over time and across raters. And, as you might expect, more specific descriptors have produced ever more reliable ratings.

Most anchored rating scales use from 5 to 9 points. Great controversies have ensued over how many points are optimal and whether it's better to have an odd or even number of points. These controversies have never been definitively resolved and most practitioners use their own experience and intuition to guide their designs. Five point scales seem to be the most widely used today. Note that virtually all such scales are Ordinal Measures as discussed back in Part 3.

For example, suppose assessors in an Assessment Center are rating a participant's "Initiative" in handling in-basket items. They have examined the actions taken and not taken on the in-basket items and now evaluate the actions on an anchored rating scale like this:

INITIATIVE

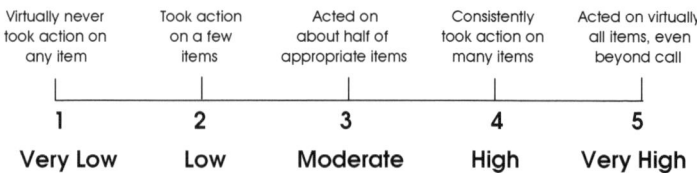

Virtually never took action on any item	Took action on a few items	Acted on about half of appropriate items	Consistently took action on many items	Acted on virtually all items, even beyond call
1	2	3	4	5
Very Low	Low	Moderate	High	Very High

The anchoring phrases are very important to the success of such ratings. Clear, simple, descriptive anchors result in easier and more reliable ratings.

The characteristic evaluated on an anchored rating scale may be quite broad (e.g., safety, national security, organizational performance) or a narrowly defined dimension of a characteristic (e.g., distribution of fire extinguishers, how well a certain statistic has been applied).

Rubrics. In some fields, rubrics are commonly used as scoring tools, especially when assessors are making evaluations in real time as evidence is being observed. A rubric is simply a matrix of rows and columns for scoring or summarizing performance. The rows are dimensions being assessed, with the cells in each row forming an anchored rating scale for that dimension. Taken as a group, then, the rows are a stack of anchored rating scales that operationalize the characteristic.

As an example, consider the task faced by judges in assessing a difficult characteristic such as "Innovative Design." How can this characteristic be operationalized and configured as a scoring rubric? One such rubric was published by the Oregon Robotics Tournament & Outreach Program (n.d.); a modified version of that rubric is shown on the following page.

RUBRIC FOR INNOVATIVE DESIGN

(adapted from Oregon Robotics Tournament & Outreach Program)

Criteria	Poor 0-4 Points	Fair 5-8 Points	Good 9-12 Points	Very Good 13-16 Points	Excellent 17-20 Points
Creativity in Design Process	Relied on building guide for all ideas. Took no risks. Relied on coach's ideas.	Relied on building guide for most ideas. Did not take risk. Did some research.	Relied on building guide for some ideas. Took minimal risks. Did research but did not implement.	Relied on building guide and also generated own ideas. Took some risks. Did research and tried to implement.	Generated many ideas. Willing to take risks. Developed design ideas from unusual sources.
Creative Design & Appearance	Standard design and appearance. No creative element. Robot has personality.	One unique item of appearance. Creative elements, but not functional. Robot has personality.	One unique item of appearance. Creative element is functional but with problems. Robot has personality.	Some uniqueness in appearance. Creative element is functional and works. Robot has personality.	Unique appearance. Creative element adds functionality. Robot has unique personality.
Uniqueness	Design copies building guide. Design often used by others. Minor differences from other robots.	Used building guide, but added elements. Design not strong, does not perform mission. Design not innovative.	Design not based on building guide. Design elements functional but not creative. Performs mission with a few problems.	Design not based on building guide. Creative design elements Performs mission. Not significantly different from others.	Design not based on building guide. Creative, innovative design significantly different from others. Performs mission reliably.
Creativity in Function	Difficulty explaining sensor use & function. No creative aspects in work, design or strategy.	Robot has sensor(s), minor difficulty explaining ideas. Robot unstable. No unusual strategy.	Robot has sensors, team can explain. Unique use of parts. Robot is stable. Unusual strategy.	Robot uses sensors, unusual parts or performs in unusual way. Creative aspects don't work as well as planned	Unique use of sensors and parts. Performs in unusual way. Creative mission approach that works.
Overall Design and Integration	No design plan or scoring strategy. No system thinking. Some elements work but not together.	Some planning, scoring strategy. Reliance on building guide. Does not achieve strategy. Little systems thinking. Most elements work, but not together.	Built to team plan, few ideas from building guide. Scoring strategy, partly achieved. Some systems thought. Elements work together, but with problems.	Built to team plan, not using building guide. Scoring strategy, present and achieved. Some systems thought. Elements work together.	Design fulfills team's plan and team's scoring strategy. Shows systems thought. Elements work together well.

This rubric uses five dimensions to operationalize the characteristic of Innovative Design—Creativity in the Design Process, Creative Design and Appearance, Uniqueness, Creativity in Function, and Overall Design and Integration. For each Dimension, five levels (from Poor to Excellent) are described. Assessors, based on the evidence they see and how it fits the scale descriptors, assign scores (1-20 points) to contestants on each of the five dimensions of Innovative Design.

Though not called rubrics, other fields use devices that are functionally equivalent to rubrics. For example, a set of evaluative descriptors—needs development, partially skilled, skilled, exceptionally skilled—have been used across a set of job performance dimensions in employee assessments. When the cells in each dimension give specific descriptions of job behaviors, this method is called a Behaviorally Anchored Rating Scale (BARS).

One issue to watch with rubrics is the temptation to mathematically average down the rows to obtain an overall evaluation. Since the dimensions are almost always ordinal measures that differ in importance, arithmetically averaging them is specious. The dimensions can be weighted to reflect their differing levels of importance, but any rigorous method for doing so is cumbersome and costly. One alternative is to have assessors examine the ratings across the dimensions and judgmentally assign an overall rating. This practice, too, has its limitations and, unfortunately, never seems quite as objective and satisfying as mathematical averaging.

Maturity Models or Maturity Ladders. Maturity Models, sometimes called Maturity Ladders, grew out of the Capability Maturity Model (Humphrey, 1988) refined in the 1980's at the Software Engineering Institute at Carnegie Mellon University. Developed to characterize how software engineering matures from chaotic efforts to a structured, disciplined process, it soon became clear that the concept could be extended to many other fields.

In assessment work, a Maturity Model can be very useful in determining and communicating the overall conclusion of an assessment. Maturity Models commonly use five stages of progress (with labels such as Initial, Ad Hoc, Planned, Managed, Optimized) to, for example, summarize the level of a program or organization being evaluated. Like an elaborate anchored rating scale, Maturity Models provide vivid, detailed descriptions of what the assessed characteristic looks like at each level. A check mark or thermometer-like bar graph can be used to display the assessed level of the characteristic.

Maturity Models offer several advantages as assessment tools. First, the points on the scale are often defined in a clearer, more detailed way than in anchored rating scales and rubrics. Second, the concept of program maturity is more descriptive and less evaluative in tone, leading to better understanding and better acceptance by the assessed entity. Third, Maturity Models are more prescriptive than other scales; the detailed descriptions of the different levels give stakeholders a clearer, and more naturalistic, picture of how an entity might move to a higher level of maturity.

The goal in constructing a Maturity Model is to paint a rich picture of the assessed characteristic at each level using, for example, descriptions of how several dimensions of the characteristic look at each level. Developing these descriptions calls for subject matter experts who can set the dimensions and describe how each dimension would mature up the ladder, much the same as with rubrics or anchored rating scales. This approach can be further refined by applying a Guttman scaling methodology to each dimension (see Trochim, 2006, for a summary on Guttman Scaling).

As a graphic example, the following figure shows an actual Maturity Model from a recent assessment project, with details obscured.

MATURITY MODEL EXAMPLE

LEVEL	DESCRIPTIVE	ASSESSED LEVEL
Optimized	Descriptive statements of Optimized level, appropriately covering observable qualities. Descriptive statements of Optimized level, appropriately covering observable qualities. Descriptive statements of Optimized level, appropriately covering observable qualities. Descriptive statements of Optimized level, appropriately covering observable qualities.	
Managed	Descriptive statements of Managed level, appropriately covering observable qualities. Descriptive statements of Managed level, appropriately covering observable qualities. Descriptive statements of Managed level, appropriately covering observable qualities. Descriptive statements of Managed level, appropriately covering observable qualities.	
Planned	Descriptive statements of Planned level, appropriately covering observable qualities. Descriptive statements of Planned level, appropriately covering observable qualities. Descriptive statements of Planned level, appropriately covering observable qualities. Descriptive statements of Planned level, appropriately covering observable qualities.	
Ad Hoc	Descriptive statements of Ad Hoc level, appropriately covering observable qualities. Descriptive statements of Ad Hoc level, appropriately covering observable qualities. Descriptive statements of Ad Hoc level, appropriately covering observable qualities. Descriptive statements of Ad Hoc level, appropriately covering observable qualities.	
Initial	Descriptive statements of Initial level, appropriately covering observable qualities. Descriptive statements of Initial level, appropriately covering observable qualities. Descriptive statements of Initial level, appropriately covering observable qualities.	

Copyright © 2010 by Measurement International. All rights reserved.

Part 8

Executing an Assessment Project

- Introduction

- Initial Preparation

- Planning & Design

- Collecting Evidence

- Analysis and Evaluation

- Report

- Continuous Improvement

Introduction

At some point, we must move from understanding assessment principles and best practices to applying them as we execute an assessment project. In previous parts of this book, we have outlined many principles and practices that lead to high quality, trustworthy assessments. Near the end of Part 5, a block diagram was used to show the stages of an assessment project. Now it's time for a more thorough outline of the work involved and our vision of how to bring an assessment from concept to conclusion.

Initial Preparation

1) **Enlist qualified assessment leader**

   - Must thoroughly understand assessment process and principles

   - Must thoroughly understand the characteristic(s) to be assessed

   - Must be independent with no conflict of interest

   - Must be able to lead/guide the assessor team

   - Familiarity with entity to be assessed is helpful

2) **Define, scope and focus the assessment**

   - Define the entity or entities to be assessed

   - Define the characteristic(s) to be assessed

   - Understand the need and purpose for the assessment

   - Examine applicable policies, rules, laws or other requirements

   - Coordinate with sponsor and entity assessed, clarifying uses of findings, concerns of sponsor, desired information and deadlines

   - Develop schedule and timeline for all assessment activities

   - Explore stakesholders' conflicting interests and any other barriers to a fair assessment

   - Set criteria for assessors to participate

3) **Enlist qualified assessors**

- Must thoroughly understand assessment principles and process, or be trained in them

- Must thoroughly understand characteristic to be assessed, or be trained accordingly

- Must be capable of teaming, with strong analytic skills and no conflict of interest

Planning & Design

4) **Specify criteria and standards, build assessment tools**

- Study relevant documents and background materials

- Choose any models or methodologies that will be used as guides

- Convene Subject Matter Experts and define the dimensions or aspects of the characteristic(s) to be assessed

- Set the types of evidence best for each characteristic or dimension

- Consult with assessment sponsor to confirm characteristic(s) and dimensions

- Construct rating scales, maturity models, interview questions, evaluation instruments, checklists, etc.

5) **Train assessor team as necessary**

- Confirm assessor capabilities

- Ensure knowledge of entity and characteristic(s) to be assessed, criteria, use of data collection tools, and assessment process

- Practice collecting and evaluating evidence

6) **Prepare for evidence collection**

- Review dimensions and evidence to be collected

- Schedule data collection and coordinate with entity being assessed

- Assign assessor tasks

Collect Evidence

7) Collect data/evidence

- Best done by assessors and/or subject matter experts

- Assessors review documents and other objective evidence, then conduct interviews and collect other qualitative data

- Seek multiple types of evidence (e.g., metrics and interviews) for each characteristic and dimension

- Assessors apply data collection instruments developed earlier, document other evidence as to source, exact quotations, etc.

- Assessors focus on data collection, studiously avoiding premature conclusions and any related discussion with other assessors

- Leader ensures consistency and independence of data collection by assessors

8) Fact Check

- Applied in certain high-quality assessments as a best practice

- Evidence is reviewed with assessed entity, providing opportunity for correction or clarification

- Supports credibility of assessment and acceptance of results; even minor factual errors can render an entire assessment less valuable

Analysis & Evaluation

9) Analyze data/evidence

- Assessors categorize evidence by characteristic or dimension

- Assessors analyze evidence, using appropriate statistics for quantitative data and Content Analysis and other means for qualitative data

10) Evaluation Session

- Assessment Leader presides and manages orderly process

- Assessors each report their evidence on one characteristic or dimension, with other assessors taking notes

- After all evidence is presented, assessors independently and privately make ratings on the characteristic or dimension, using any models, tools or rating scales

- Evaluation session proceeds similarly through remaining characteristics and dimensions

- One dimension or characteristic at a time, assessors share ratings and discuss the rating to consensus (using evidence)

- If an overall rating or evaluation is required, assessors follow the same pattern as with a characteristic or dimension

- Leader facilitates discussions and development of recommendations

- Circumstances may call for different designs to meet the same goal of independent judgments by assessors, evidence based ratings, and team consensus

- Leader is accountable for ensuring proper process throughout

115

Report

11) Report

The goal of the report is to explain the assessment methodology and results with sufficient clarity and detail that others understand and take confidence in them.

The assessment leader is accountable for the report, but may delegate various tasks.

Many report formats are workable. Most include the following:

Title Page

- Clear, descriptive title, indicating entity and characteristic(s) assessed

- Title page often includes author(s), date, and client or sponsor

Executive Summary

- Short description of assessed entity

- Purpose of assessment

- Summary of methods and analysis

- Summary of findings

- Recommendations

Introduction

- Entity, characteristics and dimensions assessed

- Scope and purpose of assessment, plus models or rationale supporting dimensions used

- Description of entity, with appropriate history

Methodology

- Assessment design and evidence collected

- Design details—sampling, methods of collecting evidence, and sources of information

- Description of any instruments, scales, etc. with reference to displays in appendices

- Issues and mitigating circumstances (sampling limitations, contaminations, etc.)

- How evaluation session was conducted

Results/Evidence

- Quantity of data collected, statistical and other analyses performed

- Tables, graphs, and illustrations necessary to show key results

Conclusions and Findings

- Positive and negative findings listed and described

- Discussion and interpretation of findings

Recommendations and Discussion

- Recommendations listed

- Appropriate explanation and discussion for each recommendation

References and Appendices

- Citations documented in reference section

- Appendices give details referenced in text

Lessons Learned

12) Collect and Document Lessons Learned

- Face-to-face meeting of assessment team, plus other stakeholders, is best

- Facilitated by Assessment Leader

- Review positives and negatives about process

- Document conclusions

Continuous Improvement

Perhaps the most fitting conclusion to our discussion here is the application of Continuous Improvement to assessments. Ongoing assessment programs typically have in place some type of improvement effort, from informal changes by the assessment manager to rather formal program reviews, corrective actions, and documented improvements. Formal or informal, all these efforts follow the familar Continuous Improvement Cycle:

CONTINUOUS IMPROVEMENT CYCLE

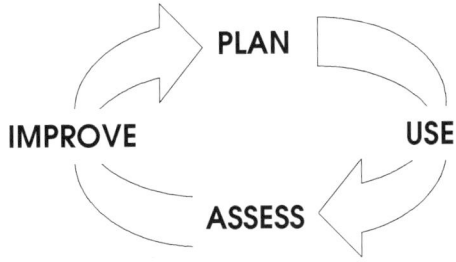

The step that makes this cycle work is the one in which new information is injected as a catalyst and basis for change— the "Assess" step.

Inputs from Lessons Learned Reviews. Where they are conducted, Lessons Learned Reviews provide a steady stream of useful input to the Continuous Improvement Cycle. These reviews were discussed in Part 5, Part 6, and in the previous section of this book.

119

The checklist provided earlier in Part 1 of this book offers questions that may be useful in a Lessons Learned Review, and other questions can be added for a more complete discussion.

Inputs from External Reviews. The other principal input to the Continuous Improvement Cycle is the External Review. In the assessment literature, an External Review is sometimes called a "meta-assessment" or "meta-evaluation"—meaning an assessment of your assessments. Assessment is a relatively immature field, and practitioners know that the most well-developed and advanced practices today will be replaced by something better tomorrow. So the input from an External Review of your practices can be quite valuable as you improve the quality of assessments.

Independent assessors are likely to use formal models in gauging your practices, models based on accepted dimensions in the literature. For example, they might use a set of anchored rating scales that follow dimensions advocated by the American Evaluation Association (n.d.), as in the following table:

DESIGN FOR EVALUATING ASSESSMENTS 1

DIMENSION	ANCHORED SCALES
– Consultation w/Stakeholders – Use of Multiple Methods – Utilization of Results – Diverse, Collaborative Assessor Teams – Cultural Sensitivity of Evaluation Practices – Effective Reporting – Independence	For each dimension, define anchor points that represent scale units such as Underdeveloped, Developing, Effective, Distinguished, etc.

Or a set of dimensions might be crafted based on the stages of an assessment effort, such as the stages outlined earlier in this section:

DESIGN FOR EVALUATING ASSESSMENTS 2

DIMENSION	ANCHORED SCALES
– Initial Preparation – Planning & Design – Evidence Collection – Analysis & Evaluation – Report – Continuous Improvement	For each dimension, define anchor points that represent scale units such as Underdeveloped, Developing, Effective, Distinguished, etc.

Practical Considerations. Continuous Improvement and the whole subject of assessment quality raise some interesting practical questions. Seeing all the ways to optimize assessments, one might reasonably ask: "How good must an

121

assessment really be?" If all assessment principles and best practices are rigorously deployed in every assessment, excessive costs will result and very few assessments will be conducted. On the other hand, if assessments are so poorly conducted that their credibility and value are called into question, the entire investment is wasted.

We believe the answer is to avoid any one-size-fits-all standard, and to adopt the guiding principles of reasonableness, balance and affordability:

- Different assessments may well call for different levels of thoroughness and rigor.

- Every assessment should be designed for optimum quality within the resources available.

- Investments should be allocated to various assessments in relation to the opportunities and risks at stake.

Concluding Remark. As we said at the outset, assessment today is a developing discipline, practiced in various ways by people in diverse fields. Our goal has been to draw lessons from those fields and set forth practices and principles for optimizing all types of assessments.

We believe the practices and principles covered here, if adopted and followed in practical, creative ways, will lead to the most accurate and useful assessments possible.

Applying these practices and principles calls for exercising judgment and experience. Our hope is that all practitioners will succeed in their best efforts to put these principles and practices to work.

Appendix A:
References & Resources

American Evaluation Association. (n.d.).
(www.eval.org)

American Evaluation Association 2003 Ethics
Committee. (2004). *Guiding principles for evaluators.*
Retrieved September 15, 2011 from: (www.eval.org/
Publications/GuidingPrinciples.asp)

American Educational Research Association, American
Psychological Association, National Council on
Measurement in Education. (1999). *Standards for
educational and psychological testing.* (ISBN-13: 978-
0935302257)

American Psychological Association. (2009).
*Assessment CyberGuide for Learning Goals and
Outcomes.* Retrieved September 15, 2011 from:
(www.apa.org/ed/governance/bea/assessment-
cyberguide-v2.pdf)

Bray, D. W., Campbell, R. J., & Grant, D. L. (1974).
*Formative Years in Business: A Long-Term AT&T
Study of Managerial Lives.* New York, NY: John Wiley
& Sons. (ISBN-13: 978-0471098102)

Bush, R. (2010, November 30). Humane Society
Outlines Concerns about Dallas Animal Shelter. *Dallas
Morning News.* Retrieved September 15, 2011 from:
(http://www.dallasnews.com/news/community-
news/dallas/headlines/20101130-humane-society-
outlines-concerns-about-dallas-animal-shelter.ece)

Cronbach L., Ambron S., Dornbusch S., Hess R., Hornik R., Phillips D., Walker D., & Weiner S. (1980). *Toward Reform of Program Evaluation: Aims, Methods and Institutional Arrangements.* San Francisco, CA: Jossey-Bass. (ISBN-13: 978-0875894713)

Department of Energy EERE Peer Review Task Force. (2004). *EERE Peer Review Guide.* Retrieved September 15, 2011 from: (www.eere.energy.gov/ba/pba/pdfs/ 2004peerreviewguide.pdf)

Energy Facility Contractors Group (EFCOG) PAAA Working Group. (2004). *Assessment Guide.* Retrieved September 15, 2011 from: (www.efcog.org/ wg/ec/docs/EFCOG%20Assessment%20Guide-Rev% 200.pdf)

Environmental Protection Agency. (2006). *Peer Review Handbook, 3rd Edition.* Retrieved September 15, 2011 from: (www.epa.gov/peerreview/pdfs/peer_review _handbook_2006.pdf)

Family Education Network. (n.d.) *The Advantages of Rubrics.* Retrieved September 15, 2011 from TeacherVision® website. (www.teachervision.fen.com/ teaching-methods-and management/rubrics/ 4522.html?detoured=1)

Frost, B. (2007). *Designing Metrics.* Dallas, TX: Measurement International. (ISBN 978-9702471-2-4)

Harrington, T. (n.d.) Quoted in Trager, 2008.

Houlihan, J. (2008). Quoted in February 29, 2008 press release by Environmental Working Group. Retrieved September 15, 2011 from: (http://www.ewg.org/release/caving-industry-pressure-epa-fires-chair-chemical-panel)

Humphrey, W. (1988). Characterizing the software process: a maturity framework. *IEEE Software*, March, 1988, 73–79.

Kaplan, R.S., & Norton, D.P. (1992). The Balanced Scorecard—Measures that Drive Performance. *Harvard Business Review*, January-February, 1992, 71-79.

Kennesaw State University. (n.d.). *Assessment Rubrics*. Retrieved September 15, 2011 from: (edtech.kennesaw.edu/intech/rubrics.htm#why)

Khattri, N., Reeve, A., & Kane, M. (1999). *Principles and practices of performance assessment*. Mahwah, NJ: Lawrence Erlham Associates. (ISBN 0-8058-2971-7)

Lunder, S., & Houlihan, J. (2008). *EPA Axes Panel Chair at Request of Chemical Industry Lobbyists*. Retrieved September 15, 2011 from Environmental Working Group website: (www.ewg.org/reports/decaconflict)

McMillan, J. H. (2000). Fundamental Assessment Principles for Teachers and School Administrators. *Practical Assessment, Research & Evaluation*, 7(8). (www.PAREonline.net/getvn.asp?v=7&n=8)

Michaels, D. (2008, July 15). It's Not the Answers That Are Biased, It's the Questions: If Two Similar Studies Completely Disagree, Look at How the Funders Framed the Issue. *Washington Post*. Retrieved September 15, 2011 from: (www.washingtonpost.com/wpdyn/content/article/2008/07/14/AR2008071402145.html)

Mlodinow, L. (2008). *The Drunkard's Walk, How Randomness Rules Our Lives.* New York: Pantheon Books. (ISBN: 978-0375424045)

Moses, J., & Byham, W. (Eds.). (1977). *The Assessment Center Method.* New York, NY: Pergamon Press. (ISBN 0-08-019581-4)

National Institute of Standards and Technology (NIST). (2011). *2011-2012 Criteria for Performance Excellence.* Retrieved September 15, 2011 from: (www.nist.gov/baldrige/publications/criteria.cfm)

Office of Management and Budget. (2003-2008). *Program Assessment Rating Tool.* Retrieved September 15, 2011 from: (www.whitehouse.gov/omb/performance_past)

Oregon Robotics Tournament & Outreach Program. (n.d.). *Innovative Design Rubric.* Retrieved September 15, 2011 from: (www.ortop.org/Innovative%20Design%20Rubric.pdf)

Stevens, S. S. (1946). On the Theory of Scales of Measurement. *Science*, June, 677–680.

127

Stufflebeam, D. L. (1999). *Evaluation Plans and Operations Checklist.* Retrieved September 15, 2011 from the Western Michigan University website: (www. wmich.edu/evalctr/wpcontent/uploads/2010/05/plan s_operations1.pdf)

Stufflebeam, D. L. (2002). *CIPP Evaluation Model Checklist.* Retrieved September 15, 2011 from the Western Michigan University website: (www.wmich. edu/evalctr/archive_checklists/cippchecklist.pdf)

Stufflebeam, D. L. (2003). *The CIPP Model for Evaluation: An update, a review of the model´s development, a checklist to guide implementation.* Paper read at Oregon Program Evaluators Network Conference, 2003. Retrieved September 15, 2011 from the Western Michigan University website: (www. wmich.edu/evalctr/pubs/CIPPModelOregon10-03.pdf)

Stufflebeam, D. L. (2004). *Evaluation Design Checklist.* Retrieved September 15, 2011 from the Western Michigan University website: (www.wmich.edu/ evalctr/archive_checklists/evaldesign.pdf)

Trager, R. (2008, March). Controversy Over EPA Removal Of Top Toxicologist. *Chemistry World.* (www.rsc.org/chemistryworld/News/2008/March/040 30801.asp)

Trochim, W. M. (2006). *Guttman Scaling.* Retrieved September 15, 2011 from the Web Center for Social Research Methods. (www. socialresearchmethods.net/kb/scalgutt.php)

Trochim, W. M. (2006). *The Research Methods Knowledge Base, 2nd Edition.* Retrieved September 15, 2011 from the Web Center for Social Research Methods. (www.socialresearchmethods.net/kb/)

United States Government Accountability Office. (2007). *Government Auditing Standards.* Retrieved September 15, 2011 from: (www.gao.gov/govaud/govaudhtml/index.html)

Worthen, B. (1990). Program evaluation. in H. Walberg & G. Haertel (Eds.), *The International Encyclopedia of Educational Evaluation* (pp. 42-47). Toronto, ON: Pergammon Press.

Final note. . .

Other books in this series include:
Measuring Performance (ISBN 0-9702471-1-7)
Crafting Strategy (ISBN 0-9702471-0-9)
Designing Metrics (ISBN 0-9702471-2-4)

Additional copies?

For quick service on multiple copies of this book or any of our other publications, call the publisher direct at 214-350-1082, or order from the website at www.MeasurementInternational.com.

22768761R00076

Made in the USA
San Bernardino, CA
20 July 2015